Mamá's Garden

by Isabella Stefan
Illustrated by Priscilla Burris

Editorial Offices: Glenview, Illinois • Parsippany, New Jersey • New York, New York
Sales Offices: Needham, Massachusetts • Duluth, Georgia • Glenview, Illinois
Coppell, Texas • Sacramento, California • Mesa, Arizona

Paula could feel the excitement in the air. She and her father were preparing for Mamá's birthday celebration. This was the Ortiz family's first spring in their own house. It had always been Mr. and Mrs. Ortiz's dream to move from their tiny apartment to a house.

Paula ran to the backyard to find Papá working in the dirt.

"My job is finished ,and yours is just beginning," said Papá, shaking the soil from his gloves. "Are the flowers ready for planting?"

"Yes, the flowers are ready. I used all the money that I saved. This will be Mamá's best birthday ever," Paula said.

---

soil: top layer of earth, dirt

"Now start planting the flowers. Mamá will be home at four o'clock," said Papá.

Papá was sorting tools for Paula to use when Paula came out of the shed. Papá was shocked.

"Paula!" Papá shouted. "What are those things?"

Papá stared at Paula's wagon filled with flowers—plastic flowers!

"But, Papá, these are just like the flowers Mamá had in our apartment," said Paula. "Mamá said that one day she would have flowers like these in her own garden."

"Oh, Paula, Paula, Paula," Papá sighed.

Just then Paula realized what she had done. "How could I have been so foolish," she cried.

---

sighed: said slowly, with a sad or tired sound

As Paula sat crying at the back fence, she noticed the beautiful flower garden in Mrs. Bailey's yard. Just then Mrs. Bailey came out her back door. "What's wrong, Paula?" she asked.

Paula then told Mrs. Bailey the story of Mamá's birthday and the plastic flowers. "Now I have no money and no real flowers," Paula sobbed.

"Come with me," said Mrs. Bailey. "I have a plan."

Paula followed Mrs. Bailey to her shed while Mrs. Bailey told Paula of her plan. Paula smiled.

Then they got to work.

At four o'clock Mamá drove into the driveway. The birthday garden was ready.

Tears filled Mamá's eyes when she saw the beautiful birthday garden. "This is the best gift I could have ever hoped for," Mamá cried. "Thank you, Paula!"

"Thank Mrs. Bailey. She gave me some of her flower seeds and helped me plant them. The plastic flowers show which kinds of flowers will grow," said Paula.